PEOPLE OF THE RAIN FOREST

RAIN FORESTS

Lynn Stone

The Rourke Corporation, Inc.
Vero Beach, Florida 32964

Printed in the U.S.A.

PHOTO CREDITS
© Breck P. Kent; cover, p. 4, 7, 8, 13; © Lynn M. Stone: title page,
p. 10, 12, 15, 17, 18, 21

Library of Congress Cataloging-in-Publication Data

Stone, Lynn M.
    People of the rain forest / by Lynn M. Stone
        p. cm. — (Discovering the rain forest)
    Includes index
    ISBN 0-86593-397-9
    1. Human Ecology—Tropics—Juvenile literature. 2. Rain forest
ecology—Tropics—Juvenile literature. 3. Indigenous peoples—
Tropics—Juvenile literature.
I. Title   II. Title: People of the rain forest.
III. Series: Stone, Lynn M. Discovering the rain forest
GF54.5.S76 1994
304.2'0911—dc20   94-20913
                                                         CIP
Printed in the USA   AC

TABLE OF CONTENTS

PEOPLE IN THE TROPICAL RAIN FORESTS

Tropical rain forests are warm, wet and wild. They are homes for countless **species**, or kinds, of plants and animals. More than one-half of the species of plants and animals on Earth live in tropical rain forests.

Rain forests are also homes for people. Small bands of **tribal** people live in some of the **remote** rain forests of South America, Southeast Asia and West Africa. These are people who have lived in the forest for hundreds, even thousands, of years.

Small bands of tribal people still live in tropical rain forest along the Amazon River of South America

TRIBAL PEOPLE

In many countries people move into cleared land in or near tropical rain forests. Most of these people farm.

A few tribal people, though, still live in the great forests themselves. These people eat monkeys, jungle birds, the honeycomb of wild bees and whatever else they can find. They use wood and leaves for their homes.

Some tribal people farm at least part-time. They grow such crops as bananas, peppers, cotton and squash.

Some tribal people of the rain forests still live with their old ways

RAIN FOREST LIVING

Native, tribal people are "in tune" with the rain forest. They respect the forest. They change the forest only slightly. Tribal people clear just enough forest to grow crops for themselves, or they clear no forest at all. They take from the forest only enough to fill their needs.

Forest tribes often move from one part of the jungle to another. The jungle soon grows over ground that they may have cleared.

Tribal people clear only enough forest for their needs

THE GREAT PROVIDER

For the tribal people who live in them, the tropical rain forests are great "providers." The rain forest provides food, medicine and shelter—all basic needs.

When governments decide to clear tropical rain forests, the native people lose their provider—and their old way of life.

Having to leave the rain forests creates many problems for native people. They are not familiar with a new way of life.

The tropical rain forest is a supermarket for tribal people

Like the creatures they study, scientists sometimes prowl the tropical rain forests at night

*Yagua warriors show visitors how to use blowguns in a
South American rain forest village*

USING THE TROPICAL RAIN FOREST

Governments have many reasons to destroy tropical rain forests, even if it means forcing native people to go elsewhere. The **lumber** from tropical rain forest trees is very valuable. Rain forests cleared for lumber can then be used for farmland, at least for a short time.

Farmers raise cattle on former rain forest lands and plant crops, such as coffee, pineapple, tea, bananas and papayas.

Governments have a continuing problem. They have to decide how much rain forest should be cleared and how much should be left alone.

Crops grow on land from which rain forest was cleared in Central America

VISITORS IN THE TROPICAL RAIN FORESTS

Native people are not the only people in tropical rain forests. Growing numbers of visitors from all over the world are arriving.

Visitors come to rain forests to see the "real jungle." They are not disappointed. The rain forests have a variety of strange and wonderful plants and animals.

Scientists come to tropical rain forests to study. They want to know how the rain forest "works" and what lives in it.

Students hike through rain forest at the La Selva Biological Research Station in Costa Rica

DISCOVERING RAIN FOREST MEDICINES

Tribal people long ago made discoveries in the tropical rain forest. They found plants that helped them cure diseases and plants that were good to eat.

Scientists today are also making discoveries in the forests. A few scientists are learning how the native people use plants as medicines.

About 100 tropical rain forest plants are now being used to make a variety of medicines.

Scientists look for new medicines by studying rain forest plants

DISCOVERING RAIN FOREST LIFE

Tropical rain forests have a remarkable number of plants and animals. Scientists are scrambling to find out just what they are! The scientists' work is a race against time. Millions of acres of tropical rain forest are being destroyed each year.

Science knows most of the rain forests' "big" animals—fish, amphibians, reptiles, birds and mammals. But millions of insects and even tinier creatures and plants are still unknown.

Some scientists think the rain forests may hold 80,000,000 kinds of insects. So far, they've identified about 500,000.

Catching a snake for a closer look is part of a wet day's work for a rain forest scientist

LA SELVA BIOLOGICAL RESEARCH STATION

One of the best study sites for tropical rain forest scientists is La Selva Biological Research Station in Costa Rica. La Selva has a modern laboratory and trails into the dark, green world of tropical rain forests.

As scientists study tropical rain forests at La Selva and elsewhere, they learn more about forest "systems." Those systems are the ways that plants, animals, air, soil and water work together.

The scientists' knowledge can help governments make wise choices about what to do with tropical rain forests.

Glossary

lumber (LUHM ber) — wood used in the building process

native (NAY tihv) — referring to people, plants or animals that are found naturally in an area, as being different from people, plants or animals that are brought into an area

remote (re MOTE) — a point far removed in distance; an out-of-the-way place

species (SPEE sheez) — a certain kind of plant or animal within a closely related group; for example, a *scarlet* macaw

tribal (TRI bull) — referring to a group of people who live in a tribe

INDEX

95585

304.2
Sto

Stone, Lynn M

People of the rain
forest

DATE DUE	BORROWER	
	Fisher	
11/10	Shan	3
5-6	Krystal Powell	22
10-15	Sabrina	4

95585

304.2
Sto

Stone, Lynn M

People of the rain
forest